A+ books

Diagrams, Diagrams, Diagrams!

by Kelly Boswell

CAPSTONE PRESS
a capstone imprint

A+ Books are published by Capstone Press,
1710 Roe Crest Drive, North Mankato, Minnesota 56003
www.capstonepub.com

Library of Congress Cataloging-in-Publication Data
Boswell, Kelly.
Diagrams, diagrams, diagrams! / by Kelly Boswell.
    pages cm. — (A+ books. Displaying information)
 Audience: K to grade 3.
 Includes index.
 ISBN 978-1-4765-0260-1 (library binding)
 ISBN 978-1-4765-3337-7 (paperback)
 ISBN 978-1-4765-3341-4 (ebook PDF)
1. Charts, diagrams, etc.—Juvenile literature. 2. Mathematical analysis—Juvenile
literature. I. Title.
 QA90.B6629 2014
 001.4'226—dc23   2012050478

Editorial Credits
Kristen Mohn, editor; Juliette Peters, designer; Marcie Spence, media researcher;
Charmaine Whitman, production specialist

Photo Credits
Capstone Press, 5, 18-19; Capstone Studio: Karon Dubke, 4, 8, 9, 10, 11, 12, 13, 14-15, 16-17,
20, 21, 22-23, 24, 25, 26, 27, 28-29; Shutterstock: Dmitry Zimin, cover (top), donatas1205,
cover (bottom), Natalia D., design element, 1, 7, 32, spfotocz, 6

Note to Parents, Teachers, and Librarians
This Displaying Information book uses full color photographs and a nonfiction format
to introduce the concept of diagrams. This book is designed to be read aloud to a
pre-reader or to be read independently by an early reader. Photographs help listeners and
early readers understand the text and concepts discussed. The book encourages further
learning by including the following sections: Table of Contents, Glossary, Read More,
Internet Sites, and Index. Early readers may need assistance using these features.

Printed in the United States of America in North Mankato, Minnesota.
032014   008072R

Table of Contents

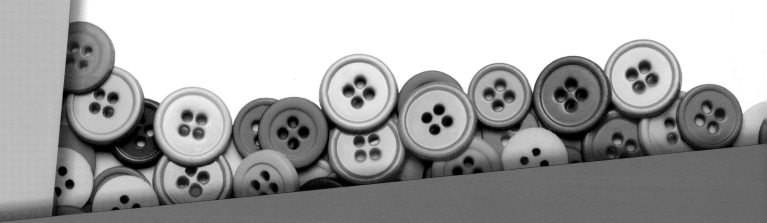

What Is a Diagram?

Head, shoulders, knees, and toes!

Kim can point to these parts on her body.

head

shoulders

knees

toes

She can also make a picture to show where each part is.

A picture that explains something is called a diagram.

A diagram can also show how parts compare to the whole.

What about the parts of a sunflower?

This sunflower has a stem and leaves.
It has petals too. Inside the flower are seeds.

We can make a diagram to show the parts of a sunflower.

Let's use art supplies to show what the sunflower looks like.

Next we add labels.

The labels tell what each part is.

Seeds

Flower

Leaves

Stem

Roots

Venn Diagrams

Kim is sorting her button collection.
She puts red buttons in this circle.

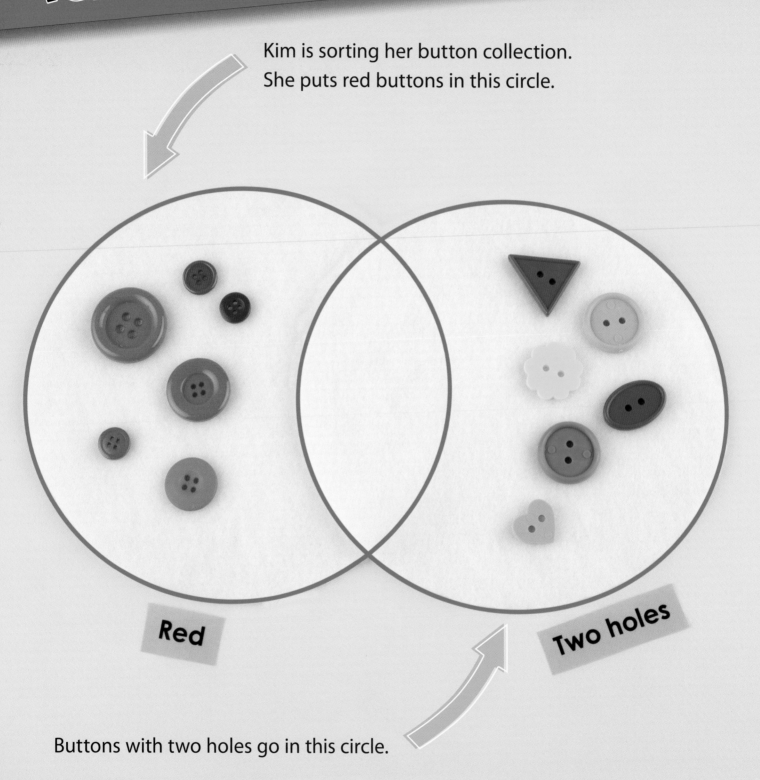

Red

Two holes

Buttons with two holes go in this circle.

Where should these buttons go?

They are red and they also have two holes. These buttons belong in both groups. They go in the shared part of the circles.

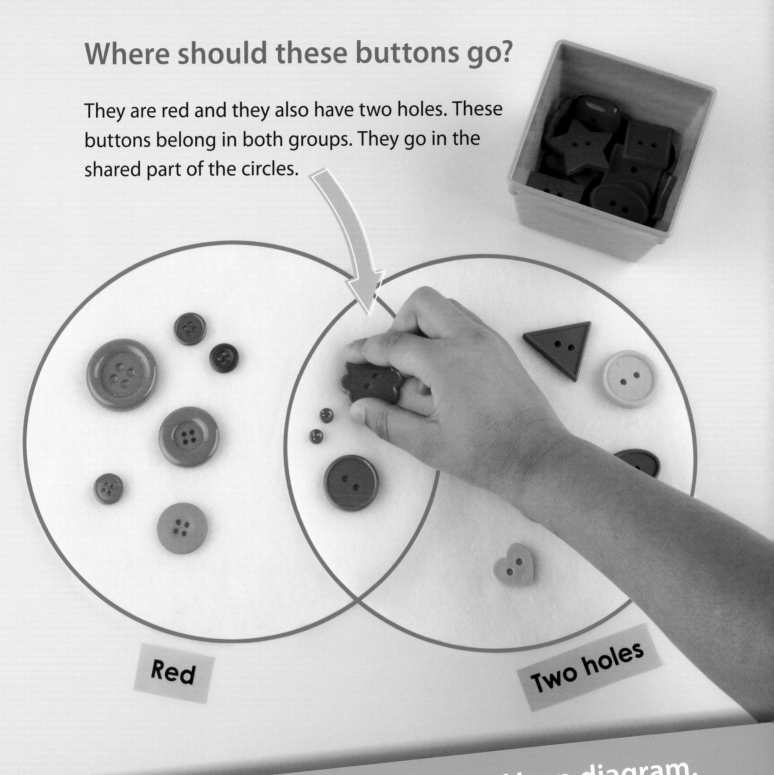

Red

Two holes

This is a kind of diagram called a Venn diagram.

Venn diagrams show what is the same and what is different.

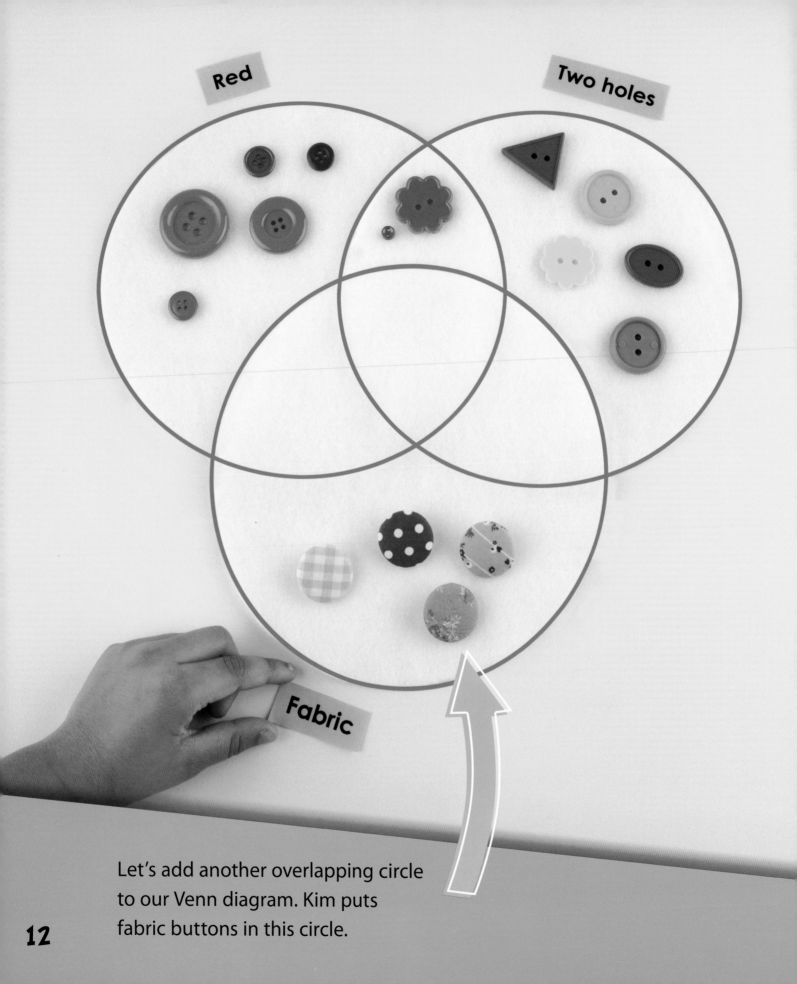

Let's add another overlapping circle
to our Venn diagram. Kim puts
fabric buttons in this circle.

Kim finds a red button that is made of fabric. It goes in the shared part of those two circles.

Here is a red button that's fabric and has two holes. This button belongs in all three groups. Kim puts it in the shared part of all three circles.

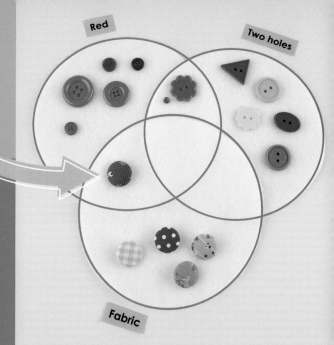

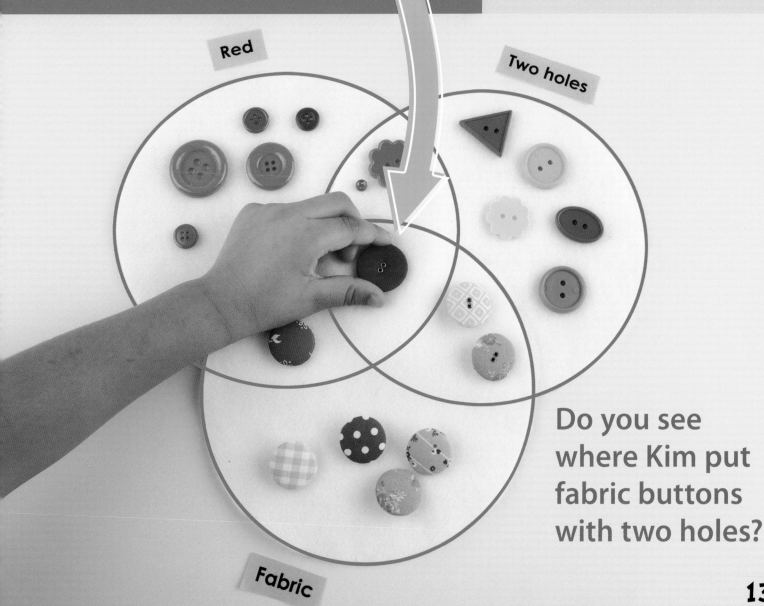

Do you see where Kim put fabric buttons with two holes?

It's fun to watch frogs!

A cycle diagram can show how a frog grows.

Cycle diagrams show what happens in a repeating process.

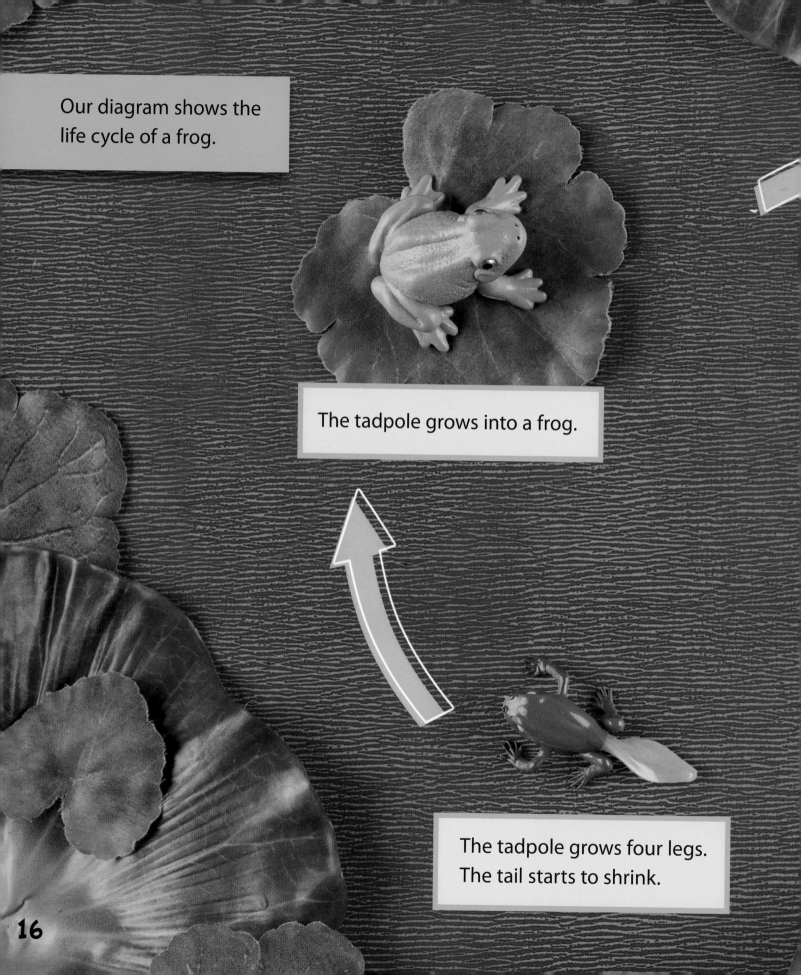

Our diagram shows the life cycle of a frog.

The tadpole grows into a frog.

The tadpole grows four legs. The tail starts to shrink.

16

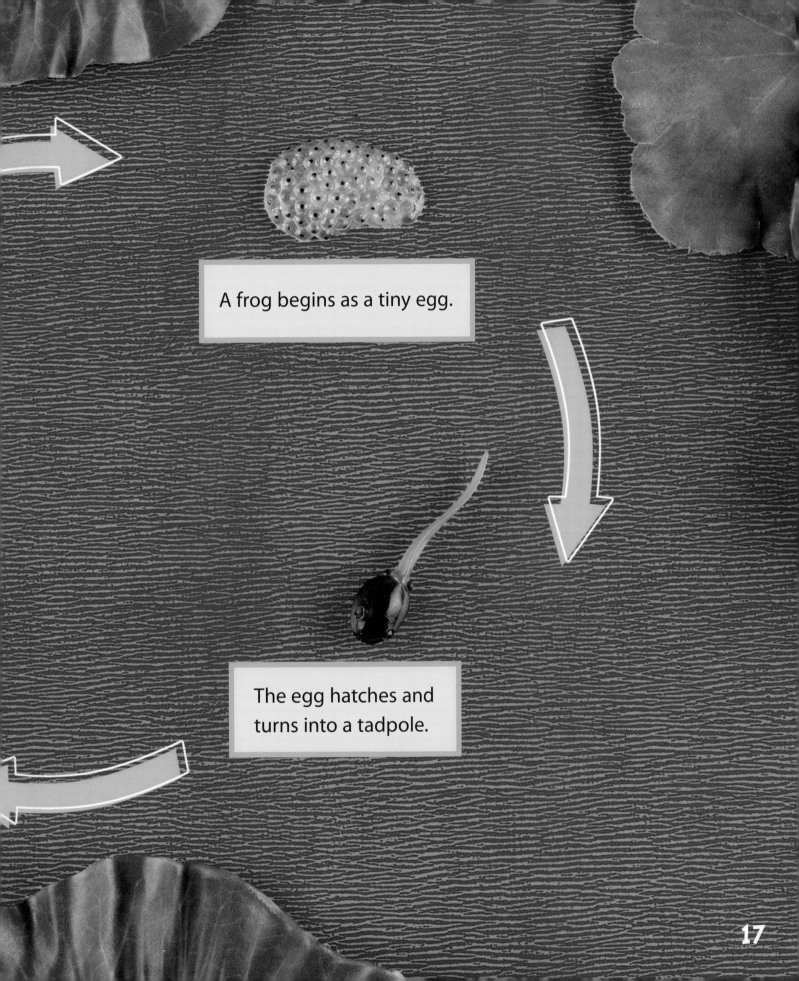

A frog begins as a tiny egg.

The egg hatches and turns into a tadpole.

The water cycle can also be shown in a cycle diagram.

Water comes down as rain or snow. Invisible droplets go back up into the sky through the air. We can see the whole water cycle in a diagram.

Flow Charts

Let's wash up!

Near the sink is a diagram called a flow chart.

A flow chart shows what events happen and in what order.

The pictures and labels remind us what to do.

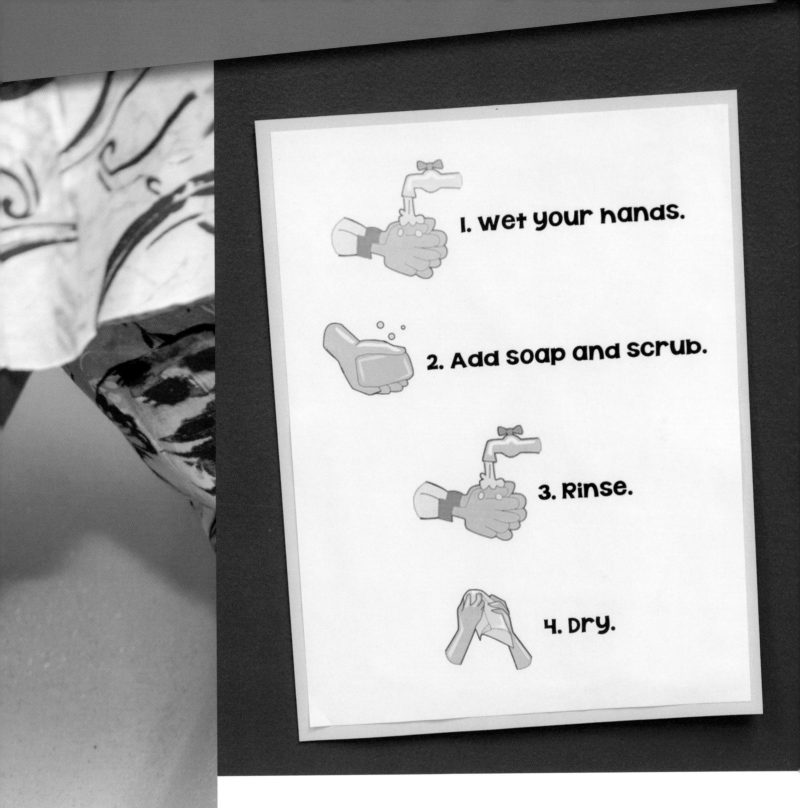

First wet your hands. Next add soap and scrub. Then rinse your hands and dry them.

All done!

Sam is hungry for a snack.

There are round crackers and square crackers. He can have cheese, peanut butter, or apples on top of his cracker.

How to decide?

A tree diagram can show
all the different choices.

23

The lines of a tree diagram look like branches on a tree.

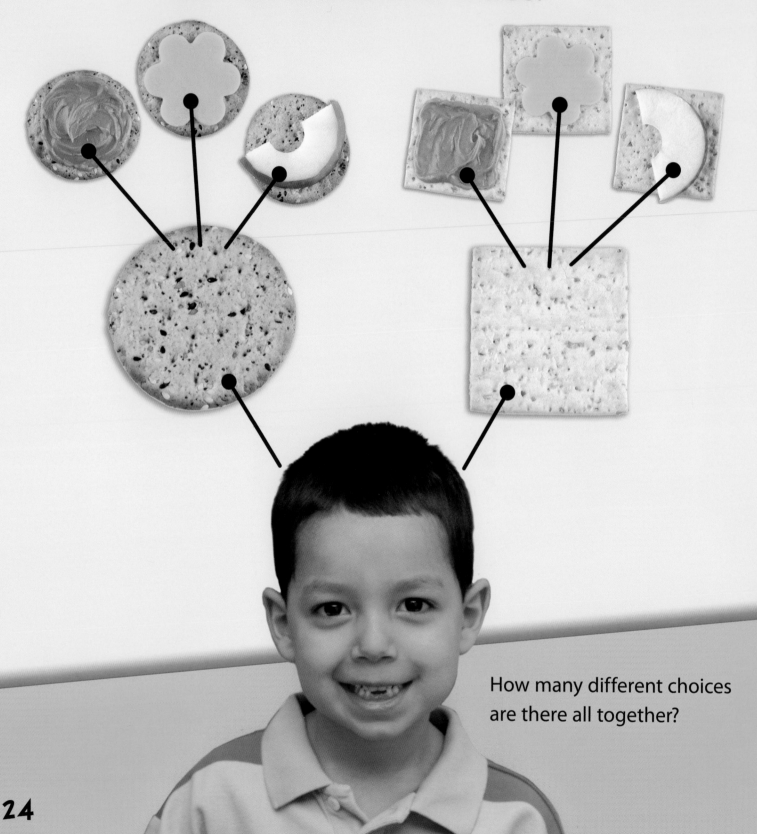

How many different choices are there all together?

Sam chooses a round cracker with cheese. **Yum!**

25

Watermelon makes a great snack too!

Let's cut into the watermelon and see what's inside. We find the rind, the fruit, and the seeds.

rind

seeds

fruit

We've made a cutaway diagram.

A cutaway diagram shows
things that are hidden inside.

Diagrams can be fun!

khees

toes

What diagrams can you make?

Glossary

cycle—a set of events that happen over and over again

diagram—a drawing that helps people understand something

label—a word on a diagram that tells what something is

process—a series of actions that creates a result

Critical Thinking Using the Common Core

1. Why do you think it's important to add labels to a diagram? (Integration of Knowledge and Ideas)

2. Compare the cycle diagrams on pages 16–17 and 18–19. What features do they have in common? How are they different? (Craft and Structure)

3. Examine the flow chart on page 21. Why do you think flow charts like this one are helpful? (Integration of Knowledge and Ideas)

Read More

Hammersmith, Craig. *The Water Cycle.* Earth and Space Science.
North Mankato, Minn.: Capstone Press, 2012.

Taylor-Butler, Christine. *Understanding Diagrams.* A True Book.
New York: Children's Press, 2013.

Thomson, Ruth. *The Life Cycle of an Oak Tree.* Learning about Life Cycles.
New York: PowerKids Press, 2009.

Internet Sites

FactHound offers a safe, fun way to find Internet sites
related to this book. All of the sites on FactHound have
been researched by our staff.

Here's all you do:

Visit *www.facthound.com*

Type in this code: 9781476502601

 **Super-cool stuff!** Check out projects, games and lots more at
www.capstonekids.com

Index